Escaping Toxic-Relationship Dynamics

the OX

and the ASS

MICHAEL A. CAPARRELLI
Ph.D (abd)

WORKBOOK

Published by UNMUTED Publications

Visit: unmuted.app
Contact: unmuted777@gmail.com

Back Cover Photo: Rebecca Daniele
(Facebook: *Radiance by Rebecca Photography)*
Book Design: wordsintheworks.com
Cover Concept: Sarah Vass

PLEASE NOTE

The OX and the Ass: Escaping Toxic-Relationship Dynamics
by Michael A. Caparrelli is now available
online and should be read ahead of this workbook.

"Michael A. Caparrelli, PhD (abd) is a prolific and prophetic writer who possesses the unique gift of communication and the ability to bring clarity to complexity. I can count on one hand preachers that possess Michael's literary and oratory skills, integrity and transparency. We, who know the man personally, recognize what an intellectual and prophetic maverick he truly is—a special gift is among us for sure."

—Bishop Jeffery A. Williams, D.Min, MPA

"Don't hesitate for one moment to welcome Michael A. Caparrelli, PhD (abd) to speak. You won't be disappointed. He is a man regenerated by the Spirit of God and wanting to convey the same to others is his passion. As a man of great character and quality, he is highly interested in people and his audiences walk away better than they arrived. Michael speaks with both humor and intellect having been highly gifted by God to serve the body of Christ in every kind of venue."

—Pasco A. Manzo President/CEO Teen Challenge New England & New Jersey

Open your eyes

Unlock your heart

Move your feet

Breaking free from toxic-relationship dynamics is as agonizing as severing one of your limbs. Contrary to what you might presume, it is not merely modifying a few behaviors; rather, it is a matter of amputating parts of your identity that have been with you since early childhood.

Whether you're cognizant of this or not, you've probably been acting out in certain behaviors that attract ASSES since you were in grade school.

People-pleasing, enabling, and other codependent tendencies have almost certainly become an integral part your personality.

So much so, that envisioning who you are without these traits seems impossible.

Breaking free from toxic relationship dynamics is *not* about liberation from someone else, but all about emancipation from the lowest parts of yourself. It is time for *you* to be set free from *you!*

Coinciding with the book, *The OX and the ASS* along with the dire need of the Holy Spirit, this workbook will accomplish three monumental tasks.

First, it will *open your eyes* to identify the dysfunctional patterns within your relationships that have depleted you of all vitality. Make no mistake about it, relationships should not be so exhausting!

Second, it will *unlock your heart* to care for yourself just as much as you cater to everyone else. Contrary to what you may think, self-care doesn't mean, *"Me First!"* It simply means, *"Me too!"*

Third, it will *move your feet* in a new direction where your relationships are synergetic experiences that draw out the best in you rather than bringing out the worst in you.

Everybody thinks that change is a wonderful idea until it's time to actually make a change! My prayer is that this workbook will translate your *wish* to change into the *will* to change. May your relationships prosper, causing you to excel like you could have never excelled riding solo.

–Michael A. Caparrelli, PhD (abd)

A Few Tips for the Journey

- Embark upon this journey simultaneously with your reading of the book, *The OX and the ASS*. Your understanding of the concepts, as well as the motivation to carry out those concepts, will not be possible without reading the book.

- Embark upon this journey with either a friend, a counselor, a pastor or a network of people who can help you stay accountable to the truths you discover.

- Keep the focus on *you* and *your role* rather than your partner throughout this journey. Of course, you will naturally become awakened to the damage that someone else may be causing in your life. However, do not use this book as a billy club to beat on them, but use it as a mirror to look at yourself.

- Pray throughout your journey, asking for the Holy Spirit to assist you in this process of transformation.

- Conduct a Bible study on the verses referenced throughout this journey, allowing the Word of God to enlighten and empower you.

- Before making any major decisions such as separation or divorce, please talk it over with a pastor, a counselor or a trusted advisor.

- Spend one thoughtful week on each chapter and lesson rather than breezing through the book and workbook in a few sittings.

- Important: If you are in an abusive situation where you are in danger, please contact the following phone number to seek advice. Call **1-800-799-7233** today to speak with an advocate who can assist you.

Lesson 1:
Unequally Yoked Relationships

1. Read Deuteronomy 22:10. What are the consequences of being in unequally yoked relationships? What consequences have you suffered personally, if any?

_____

_____

_____

_____

_____

_____

_____

_____

_____

_____

_____

_____

_____

_____

_____

_____

_____

_____

_____

_____

2. Are you an OX? Place a check-mark next to every trait that applies.

_____If you're sensitive to the needs of others, you might be an OX.

_____If you enjoy serving more than being served, you might be an OX.

_____If you easily take responsibility for other people's issues, you might be an OX.

_____If you initiate most of what happens in your relationships, you might be an OX.

_____If you perceive your sacrifices for others as a privilege, you might be an OX.

_____If disloyalty or dishonesty crushes you, you might be an OX.

_____If you are generous with your time, talents and resources, you might be an OX.

_____If you have the potential of being an enabler/codependent, you might be an OX.

_____If you're drawn to ASSES (as described on page 18), you might be an OX.

3. Elaborate on the Four A Circles. How have you been affected by these circles?

The Circle of Addiction

_____

_____

_____

_____

_____

The Circle of Abuse

The Circle of Adultery

The Circle of Abandonment

4. Are you in a relationship with anyone that fits *The Profile of an ASS?* (Or maybe you fit *The Profile of an ASS?*)

_____If he/she is a habitual offender with one of the Four A Circles, you might be with an ASS

_____ If he/she has a propensity to blame others for what's wrong, you might be with an ASS.

_____ If he/she hates being inconvenienced or going out of their way, you might be with an ASS.

_____ If he/she is defensive about their defects, you might be with an ASS.

_____ If he/she is closed to the idea of therapy regarding their issues, you might be with an ASS.

_____ If he/she lacks the energy to invest in your relationship, you might be with an ASS.

_____ If he/she mulls over their own feelings more than others, you might be with an ASS.

_____ If he/she is drawn to OXEN (as described previously), you might be with an ASS.

5. For *married people*, please read I Corinthians 7:12-15 to understand the value of staying in a relationship with an ASS. However, please seek counsel from a pastor, a counselor and/or a trusted advisor if your safety is in jeopardy. Elaborate below on the counsel you received as well as your own personal thoughts.

_____

_____

_____

_____

_____

_____

_____

_____

_____

_____

_____

_____

_____

_____

_____

_____

_____

_____

_____

_____

_____

_____

6. For *single people,* please re-read Deuteronomy 22:10 & II Corinthians 6:14, the story of Samson and Delilah in Judges 16, and "The OX and the ASS" in its entirety before entering into a covenant with an ASS. Elaborate below on the characteristics that are important to you in a mate.

_____

_____

_____

_____

Lesson 2: The Yokes

1. Read II Corinthians 6:14. What does "yoke" mean to you based on your experiences?

_____

_____

_____

_____

_____

_____

_____

_____

_____

_____

_____

_____

_____

_____

_____

_____

_____

_____

2. Have you been addicted to love? Check off the symptoms that apply to you.

_____You lose self-control when triggered by your partner (Read I Cor. 13:5).

_____You have no life outside the relationship (Read I Cor. 13:4).

_____You endure a continual break-up and make-up cycle (Read I Cor. 13:4).

_____You rely upon sex for love (Read I Cor.13:5).

_____You experience non-stop thinking about the relationship (Read I Cor. 13:6).

_____You act in ways that contravene your beliefs, morals and ethics. (Read I Cor. 13:6).

_____You experience low self-esteem when triggered by your partner (Read I Cor. 13:4)

_____You are fully invested in a relationship that doesn't give you a satisfactory Return On Investment, a.k.a., R.O.I.

3. Elaborate on how one of the following yokes have applied to you, if any at all.

The Yoke of Chemicals

_____

_____

_____

_____

The Yoke of Control

The Yoke of Convenience

The Yoke of Co-dependency

4. Read about the relationship between Pharaoh and the people in Exodus 5 and Exodus 16. Are there any Pharaohs in your life? How have you been yoked to them?

_____

_____

_____

_____

_____

_____

_____

_____

_____

_____

_____

_____

_____

_____

_____

_____

5. If you are married, elaborate on the ways you are yoked to your spouse: good, bad or indifferent? Base your answers on the content of this chapter or other unmentioned yokes.

_____

_____

_____

_____

_____

_____

_____

_____

_____

_____

_____

_____

_____

_____

_____

_____

_____

_____

_____

_____

_____

6. If you are single, which of these yokes are you most susceptible to base on your childhood and adulthood experiences?

_____

_____

_____

_____

_____

_____

_____

_____

Lesson 3: Eat Healthy

1. Read Deuteronomy 25:4. Elaborate on the recipe for burn-out in a relationship. Share about any experiences you have had with burnout?

_____
_____
_____
_____
_____
_____
_____
_____
_____
_____
_____
_____
_____
_____
_____
_____
_____
_____
_____

2. Psychological breakdowns happen when you spend more time with people who *need* you rather than *feed* you. List the people who *need* you and the people who *feed* you.

People who *need* you:

_____

_____

_____

_____

_____

_____

_____

_____

_____

_____

People who *feed* you:

_____

_____

_____

_____

_____

_____

_____

_____

_____

_____

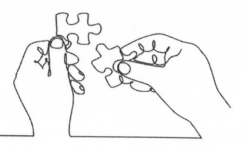

3. The "Eat Healthy" Challenge.

- Meditate upon one of the recommended Bible passages, along with your own preferred passages, for 15 minutes every morning and 15 minutes every night for this week.

- Start reading one of the three recommended books from the survey section on pages 55 and 56 of *The OX and the ASS*."

- Log below some of the "Truth-Nutrients" you have meditated upon this week. If you are married, in what ways did these "Truth-Nutrients" empower you to break free from toxic-relationship dynamics? If you are single, in what ways did these "Truth- Nutrients" help you gain leverage over your own toxic feelings?

Day 1: Truth-Nutrients

_____
_____
_____
_____
_____
_____
_____
_____
_____

Day 2: Truth-Nutrients

_____
_____
_____
_____
_____
_____
_____
_____
_____
_____
_____
_____
_____
_____

Day 3: Truth-Nutrients

_____
_____
_____
_____
_____
_____
_____
_____
_____
_____
_____
_____

Day 4: Truth-Nutrients

_____

_____

_____

_____

_____

_____

_____

_____

_____

_____

_____

_____

Day 5: Truth-Nutrients

_____

_____

_____

_____

_____

_____

_____

_____

_____

_____

_____

_____

_____

_____

_____

Day 6: Truth-Nutrients

_____
_____
_____
_____
_____
_____
_____
_____
_____
_____
_____
_____

Day 7: Truth-Nutrients

_____
_____
_____
_____
_____
_____
_____
_____
_____
_____
_____
_____:
_____

Lesson 4: Carry Your Loads

1. 1.Read Galatians 6:6. Share about the significance of this verse for you personally.

_____

_____

_____

_____

_____

_____

_____

_____

_____

_____

_____

_____

_____

_____

_____

_____

_____

_____

_____

2. What are the "incentives" that keep you yoked to people? Consider the following and comment on what applies to you.

My Partner is my Pal.

_____

_____

_____

_____

_____

_____

_____

_____

_____

_____

_____

_____

_____

_____

_____

_____

_____

My Partner is my Provider.

_____

_____

My Partner is my Lover.

My Partner is my Scapegoat.

My Partner is my Servant.

3. How are you learning to "carry your own load"? How do you anticipate your new autonomy affecting your relationships?

_____

_____

_____

_____

_____

_____

_____

_____

_____

_____

_____

_____

_____

_____

_____

_____

_____

_____

_____

_____

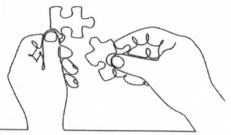

4. The "Carry Your Load" Challenge.

- Identify the list of incentives (a.k.a., bait) that keeps you stuck in this relationship. If you are single, what incentives keep you stuck in other toxic relationships (such as parents, siblings, friends, etc.)?

- Talk over with your therapist, pastor or trusted friend these incentives and how to break free from such a yoke. After the talk, what are some things you discovered?

- Learn to carry your own load within these areas. Make strides towards independence in these areas, learning to stand on your own feet. Comment on the strides you made this week.

- Anticipate a weaning process whereby you experience withdrawal-symptoms by not looking to your partner anymore in that area. Elaborate on the symptoms you experienced this week, if any.

_____

_____

_____

_____

_____

_____

_____

_____

_____

Lesson 5: Use Your Horns

1. Read Numbers 23:22. Expound upon what this verse means to you personally.

_____

_____

_____

_____

_____

_____

_____

_____

_____

_____

_____

_____

_____

_____

_____

_____

_____

_____

_____

_____

_____

_____

_____

2. Elaborate on the ways you have been an "easy mark." Share about the stuff you've picked up that's not yours.

_____

_____

_____

_____

_____

_____

_____

_____

_____

_____

_____

_____

_____

_____

_____

_____

_____

3. True or False. "I Go Along To Get Along." If true, share about what that has cost you?

_____

_____

_____

_____

_____

_____

_____

_____

_____

_____

_____

_____

_____

_____

_____

_____

_____

_____

_____

4. Identify the "pearls" in your life worth protecting (Matthew 7:6). Consider the following list.

_____Your Trust (Matthew 7:16)

_____Your Time (Ephesians 5:16)

_____Your Thoughts and Feelings (Proverbs 4:23)

_____Your Sexuality (I Corinthians 6:19-20)

_____Your Purpose (Romans 8:30-31)

_____Your Relationship with God (I John 3:7)

_____Your Relationship with Others (Philippians 2:3)

_____Your Morals and Values (Psalm 1:1)

_____Your Possessions (Proverbs 3:9)

_____Your Name (Proverbs 22:1)

5. Which of the following areas do you struggle with? Check them off and work on those areas this week.

_____Identify the Pearls of Your Life (Matthew 7:6)

_____Tune Into Your Spirit (I Corinthians 14:33)

_____Determine The Boundary Lines (Psalm 16:6)

_____Determine the Consequences (Matthew 18:17)

_____Say What You Mean (Matthew 5:33)

_____Mean What You Say (Matthew 5:37)

_____Don't Say It Mean (Ephesians 4:15)

_____Don't Pick Up What's Not Yours (Proverbs 4:23)

_____Assume His Yoke Alone (Matthew 11:30)

_____Yoke with Other Oxen (Proverbs 27:17)

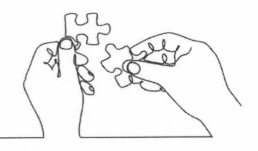

6. *The "Use Your Horns" Challenge.*

- List your pearls (above).

- Share your boundaries as well as the ensuing consequences for crossing them.

- Seek counsel from a trusted person on relaying those boundaries to the ASSES. Elaborate on the counsel they gave you.

- Practice using your horns with a trusted person by role-playing. Share about your experiences.

- Ask a trusted person to hold you accountable to the boundaries you lay out. Who is this person and how will they hold you accountable?

Lesson 6:
Stay Close to the Herd

1. Read Ecclesiastes 4:9-12. Describe the people within your "herd."

_____

_____

_____

_____

_____

_____

_____

_____

_____

_____

_____

_____

_____

_____

_____

_____

_____

_____

_____

2. Comment on how your herd-relationships provide the following benefits for you.

Accountability: "Two are better than one because they have a good return for their labor" (Ecclesiastes 4:9).

_____

_____

_____

_____

_____

_____

_____

_____

_____

_____

_____

Advocacy: "If either of them falls down, one can help the other up. But pity anyone who falls and has no one to help them up" (Ecclesiastes 4:10).

_____

_____

_____

_____

_____

_____

_____

_____

_____

_____

_____

Comradery: "If two lie down together, they will keep warm. But how can one can warm alone" (Ecclesiastes 4:11).

_____

_____

_____

_____

_____

_____

_____

_____

_____

_____

_____

Safety: "Though one may be overpowered, two can defend themselves" (Ecclesiastes 4:12).

_____

_____

_____

_____

_____

_____

_____

_____

_____

_____

_____

_____

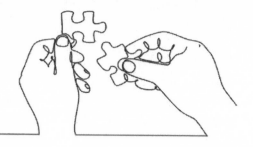

3. "Stay Close to the Herd" Challenge.

- Seek for outside support by seeing a therapist, joining a support group (such as Al Anon) and becoming a part of a church family. Comment on your experiences with that herd this week.

- Meet with someone you trust on a regular basis on the telephone, out for coffee or wherever you feel comfortable. Comment on your experiences with that person this week.

- Don't just SHOW UP but OPEN UP! Allow that trusted person into the private areas of your life. Share with them about your struggles in this relationship. Share about your experiences of OPENING UP this week.

Lesson 7: Pen Up

1. Read Exodus 21:36. Share about what this verse means to you personally.

_____

_____

_____

_____

_____

_____

_____

_____

_____

_____

_____

_____

_____

_____

_____

_____

_____

_____

_____

_____

_____

2. What are your indications that it's time for you to PEN UP?

_____

_____

_____

_____

_____

_____

_____

_____

_____

_____

_____

_____

_____

_____

_____

_____

_____

_____

3. Which pens do you use? Comment on how these pens alleviate your stress.

A Natural Setting

_____

_____

_____

_____

_____

A Visit with Your Friend

_____

_____

_____

_____

_____

_____

Church Long Drives in Your Car

_____

_____

_____

_____

_____

_____

Nostalgic Places

_____

_____

_____

_____

_____

_____

The Bathroom

_____

_____

_____

_____

_____

_____

Other

_____

_____

_____

_____

_____

4. The Pen Up Challenge.

- Find a Pen that fits the following criteria—some distance from your warzone, connotes feelings of safety, remains secretive and is easily accessible. Elaborate on that place.

- Frequent your Pen at least three times this week, and/or every time you feel fed up. Elaborate on how that place helped you alleviate stress from your relationships.

Lesson 8:
Do What's Under Your Nose

1. Read Matthew 11:30. Share about. What does this verse mean to you personally?

_____

_____

_____

_____

_____

_____

_____

_____

_____

_____

_____

_____

_____

_____

_____

_____

_____

_____

2. Check off any OVER-YOUR-HEAD situations you're stressing about within your relationships. Comment at bottom on whatever applies to you.

_____Other's reactions

_____Other's perception of you

_____Past events

_____Future events

_____Sickness or death

_____Money you don't have

_____Physical or mental handicaps

_____Being alone

_____Nature

_____Your personality

_____

_____

_____

_____

_____

_____

_____

_____

_____

_____

_____

_____

_____

_____

_____

_____

_____

_____

_____

_____

_____

_____

_____

_____

_____

_____

_____

_____

_____

_____

_____

3. Based on research, and the words of Jesus in Matthew 6:25-34, what can we determine about worry?

_____

_____

_____

_____

_____

_____

_____

_____

_____

4. Comment on how managing the UNDER-YOUR-NOSE areas listed below help you break free within your relationships.

How you treat others

_____

_____

_____

_____

_____

_____

How you perceive situations

_____

_____

_____

_____

_____

How you react to people, places and things

_____

_____

_____

_____

_____

The places you go

_____

_____

_____

_____

_____

_____

The people you visit

_____

_____

_____

_____

_____

The things you digest

_____

_____

_____

_____

_____

The help you seek or don't seek

_____

_____

_____

_____

_____

Your thoughts

_____

_____

_____

_____

Your words

_____
_____
_____
_____
_____
_____

How you spend your resources (including time)

_____
_____
_____
_____
_____
_____

5. The "Do-What's-Under-Your-Nose" Challenge.

- List up to ten things of the stuff that's "UNDER-YOUR-NOSE" and the stuff "OVER-YOUR-HEAD"

  Under-my-nose

  _____
  _____
  _____

_____

_____

_____

_____

_____

_____

_____

_____

Over-my-head

_____

_____

_____

_____

_____

_____

_____

_____

_____

- Say the "Serenity Prayer" in the morning before you head out and at night before you go to sleep. Comment on how you feel as you recite that prayer.

_____

_____

_____

_____

_____

_____

_____

_____

_____

- When you worry about your relationships, jot down the object of that worry below. Next, cross-out all the objects that are OVER-YOUR-HEAD.

_____

_____

_____

_____

_____

_____

_____

_____

_____

- As you manage the stuff UNDER-YOUR-NOSE, jot down any progress you observe this week related to that stuff; internal and circumstantial progress.

_____

_____

_____

_____

_____

_____

_____

_____

_____

_____

Lesson 9:
Outgrow Your Oppressor

1. Read Isaiah 10:27. Elaborate on what this verse means to you personally.

_____

_____

_____

_____

_____

_____

_____

_____

_____

_____

_____

_____

_____

_____

_____

_____

_____

_____

_____

_____

_____

2. Are there relationships within your life stifling you from growth? If so, please elaborate.

_____

_____

_____

_____

_____

_____

_____

_____

_____

_____

_____

_____

_____

_____

_____

_____

_____

_____

3. Elaborate on the areas of personal development relevant to you.

Enroll in a course

_____

_____

_____

_____

_____

_____

Join the gym

_____
_____
_____
_____
_____
_____
_____

Become a member of a church family

_____
_____
_____
_____
_____
_____
_____

Attend a support group

_____
_____
_____
_____
_____
_____
_____

Find a therapist

_____
_____
_____
_____

_____

_____

_____

Go on a Missions trip

_____

_____

_____

_____

_____

_____

Take up a hobby like fishing, dancing, learning a language, etc.

_____

_____

_____

_____

_____

_____

Other

_____

_____

_____

_____

_____

_____

_____

4. Expound upon the effects that your growth has on the people within your life.

Your Growth MOTIVATES them.

_____

_____

_____

_____

_____

_____

_____

_____

Your Growth INFURIATES them.

_____

_____

_____

_____

_____

_____

_____

Your Growth ELIMINATES them.

_____

_____

_____

_____

_____

_____

_____

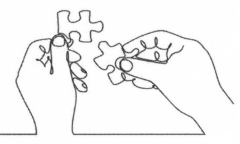

5. The "Outgrow Your Oppressor" Challenge.

- Work on 1 area of personal development this week. Elaborate on your experiences.

- Notice how your growth affects your relationships. Share your experiences.

- Resist any potential backlash from others as you advance forward.

Lesson 10: Nurse Your Wounds

1. Read Psalm 147:3. Elaborate on what this verse means to you personally.

_____

_____

_____

_____

_____

_____

_____

_____

_____

_____

_____

_____

_____

_____

_____

_____

_____

_____

_____

_____

_____

2. Share about your experiences with any of the Narcissists listed within the book.

Anti-Social Narcissist

_____
_____
_____
_____
_____
_____
_____
_____
_____
_____
_____
_____
_____
_____
_____
_____
_____
_____
_____

Vulnerable Narcissist

_____
_____
_____
_____
_____
_____

Charismatic Narcissist

_____

_____

Malignant Narcissist

_____

_____

_____

_____

_____

_____

_____

_____

_____

_____

_____

_____

_____

_____

_____

_____

_____

_____

_____

_____

3. Elaborate upon one or more of the following six wounds that makes you easy prey if not nursed properly.

Broken Trust

_____

_____

_____

_____

_____

_____

_____

_____

_____

_____

_____

_____

_____

_____

_____

_____

_____

_____

_____

_____

Shattered Self-image

_____

_____

_____

_____

_____

_____

_____

_____

_____

_____

_____

_____

_____

_____

_____

_____

_____
_____
_____
_____
_____

Weakened Self-efficacy

_____
_____
_____
_____
_____
_____
_____
_____
_____
_____
_____
_____
_____
_____
_____
_____
_____
_____

Post-Traumatic Stress

_____
_____
_____
_____

Disease of Resentment

_____

_____

_____

_____

_____

Early Childhood Wounds

_____

_____

_____

_____

_____

_____

_____

_____

_____

_____

_____

_____

_____

_____

_____

_____

_____

7. Share about the remedies you applied for any of the selected wounds.

_____

_____

_____

_____

_____

_____

_____

_____

_____

_____

_____

_____

_____

_____

_____

_____

8. The "Nurse Your Wounds" Challenge.

- Ask someone from your herd to identify your wound(s). Share their feedback here.

- Apply 1 or more of the remedies appropriate to that wound listed within the book. Share about your experiences here.

- Take some space from any of the identified narcissists within your life (if any) when needed, especially when feeling fragile.

Lesson 11: Know Your Owner

1. Read Isaiah 1:3. Share about what this verse means to you personally.

_____

_____

_____

_____

_____

_____

_____

_____

_____

_____

_____

_____

_____

_____

_____

_____

_____

_____

_____

_____

_____

2. Comment on any of the methods of control that have been used on you by someone.

Fear Tactics

_____

_____

_____

_____

_____

_____

_____

Guilt Trips

_____

_____

_____

_____

_____

_____

False Alarms

_____

_____

_____

_____

_____

_____

_____

_____

_____

_____

_____

_____

_____

_____

3. How does knowing your owner keep you from being controlled by someone else?

_____

_____

_____

_____

_____

_____

_____

_____

_____

_____

_____

_____

_____

_____

_____

_____

_____

_____

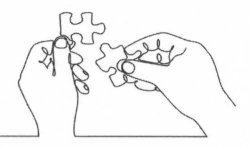

4. The "Know Your Owner" Challenge.

- Build your relationship with your Owner through spending 15 minutes every day this week in prayer and reading the Word of God. Share about your experiences here.

- Develop your relationship with your Owner by acknowledging Him in all your decisions. Before you commit to help anyone, take some time to pray. Practice the habit of telling people, "Give me some time to think and pray about that request before I say yes."

- Resist all methods of control this week, reminding yourself of your true owner. Share about your experiences below.

Lesson 12:
Dodging Wild ASSES

1. Read Genesis 16:12. Elaborate on what this verse means to you.

_____

_____

_____

_____

_____

_____

_____

_____

_____

_____

_____

_____

_____

_____

_____

_____

_____

_____

_____

_____

_____

_____

2. Comment on any of the unleashed fury you have experienced listed below.

Manipulation

_____
_____
_____
_____
_____
_____
_____

Accusation

_____
_____
_____
_____
_____
_____
_____

Villainization

_____
_____
_____
_____
_____
_____

Intimidation

_____
_____
_____
_____
_____
_____
_____

3. Elaborate upon the three muscles required to dodge wild ASSES.

The Horn Muscle

_____
_____
_____
_____
_____
_____
_____
_____

The Empathy Muscle

_____
_____
_____
_____
_____
_____
_____

_____

_____

_____

_____

_____

_____

_____

_____

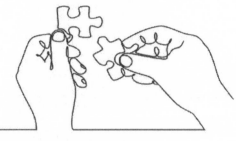

4. The "Dodge Wild ASSES" Challenge.

- *The Horn Muscle* - Enforce necessary boundaries that match their fury. For instance, if the Wild Ass attacks you on social media, block him/her. If they threaten your life, file for a restraining order. Share about your experiences.

- *The Empathy Muscle* - Empathize with their situation. Once again, this does not mean extending sympathy. It simply means discerning their handicaps in order to forgive them for their cruelty. Share about your experiences.

- *The Ignore Muscle* - Keep Shining! Go after your goals while prohibiting the Wild Asses from derailing you from your destiny. Share about your experiences.

Lesson 13: Mating With OXEN

1. Read Job 1:14. Elaborate on what this verse means to you.

_____
_____
_____
_____
_____
_____
_____
_____
_____
_____
_____
_____
_____
_____
_____
_____
_____
_____
_____
_____
_____
_____

2. Expound upon the synergetic relationships within your life.

_____

_____

_____

_____

_____

_____

_____

_____

_____

_____

_____

_____

_____

_____

_____

_____

_____

_____

_____

3. Expound upon your understanding of the following tests when determining if someone is the right match.

The Healthy Test

_____

_____

_____

_____

_____

_____

_____

_____

_____

_____

_____

_____

_____

_____

_____

_____

_____

The Energy Test

_____

_____

_____

_____

_____

_____

_____

_____

_____

_____

_____

_____

_____

_____

_____

_____

_____

The Adversity Test

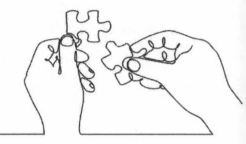

4. The "Mate With An OX" Challenge.

If you are contemplating a relationship with someone, apply these tests.
Comment on your experiences with that person related to each test.

The Healthy Test

_____

_____

_____

_____

_____

_____

_____

_____

_____

_____

_____

_____

_____

_____

_____

_____

_____

_____

_____

_____

The Energy Test

_____
_____
_____
_____
_____
_____
_____
_____
_____
_____
_____
_____
_____
_____
_____
_____
_____
_____
_____
_____
_____

The Adversity Test

_____
_____
_____
_____
_____
_____
_____
_____

About the Author

Michael A. Caparrelli, PhD (abd) served for sixteen years as a pastor of a recovery church in Rhode Island. Currently, he is in the final dissertation stage of his PhD in Behavioral Science, investigating the impact of church on the recovery journey of adults with addictions.

He travels across the nation, speaking to churches, schools, prisons and rehabs, on a variety of subjects in behavioral health from a faith-based perspective.

He also is an adjunct professor of psychology at Northpoint College and author of the well-received *Pen Your Pain Into Parables*.

He has four children–Ashley, Mikie, Hannah and Olivia. He is a devout follower of Jesus Christ.

If you would like to book Michael for a speaking engagement,
please email him at: Michaelcaparrelli@unmuted.app

Acknowledgements

First and foremost, I give praise and thanksgiving to my Lord and Savior, Jesus Christ, for keeping me stable and productive during some very trying times.

To all of my mentors, my spiritual Father, Pastor Pat Manzo, my coach in the corner, Bishop Jeff Williams, my pastor, Tony Palow, the man who discipled me, Pastor Scott Axtmann and my business mentor and close friend, Matt Olerio, my spiritual moms, Jacqui Strothoff, Jen Tufano & Iris Pelley, you encouraged me beyond all of my insecurities and helped me find my dreams right on the other side of my fears.

To my children, Ashley, Mikie, Hannah and Olivia, allow God to map out your life, especially the picking of your mate. God knows what you desire and require far better than you do. I love and adore each of you, and you make my life complete.

To Joe Cannistraci, you were the one who invested in my spiritual formation when I was just a young Bible college student with not a penny in my pocket.

To John Stebbene, you saved my life this year and have always been a friend to lean on.

To my sweetheart Alicia, you are the OX who inspired this book. I love you and admire all of the virtues you so effortlessly exhibit.

And with thanks to:

Words in the Works for the production of this book:
www.wordsintheworks.com

Sarah Vass for the *OX and ASS* cover concept.

Rebecca Danielle and *Radiance by Rebecca Photography* at:
www.facebook.com/RRPhotography616/

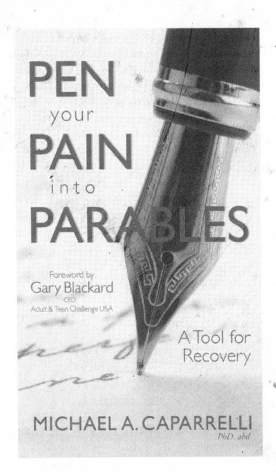

Out of his own past along with a higher education in behavioral science, Michael A. Caparrelli, PhD (abd) helps you frame the painful moments of yours—the annoyances and the grievances, the losses and divorces, the abuse and the misuse, the rejection and depression—in a manner that transforms your story into the greatest asset you have.

By the end of *Pen Your Pain Into Parables*, you will no longer be emotionally crippled by the people, places and things of yesteryear. At one time, your past was an anchor that dragged you downward. After you pen your pain into parables, your past will become a rudder that guides them forward.

Accompanying workbook also available

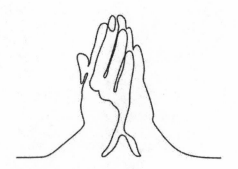